CATECHISM FOR THEOLOGIANS

The Foundations For Meaningful Jewish/Christian Dialogue

John McGinley

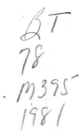

UNIVERSITY
PRESS OF
AMERICA

Copyright © 1981 by
University Press of America, Inc.™
P.O. Box 19101, Washington, D.C. 20036

Printed in the United States of America

ISBN: 0-8191-1595-9

Library of Congress Number: 81-40063

Man was created not to know happiness but
truth. To discover it, one must start anew;
everything must be reviewed. Man, chosen by God,
must choose Him in turn. All ready-made answers,
all seemingly unalterable certainties serve only
to provide a good conscience to those who like
to sleep and live peaceably. To avoid spending
a lifetime tracking down truth, one pretends to
have found it. But, so one says in Kotzk,
revelation itself, once it has become a habit
and a front, becomes suspect.

                                    Elie Wiesel

                                    Souls on Fire

Preface

This study started out to be a commentary
on Schelling's Ages of the World. But the actual
writing of the commentary turned itself, by itself
as it were, into an integration of Ages of the
World into a theological brief which in many
crucial ways is decidedly un-Schellingesque.
Nonetheless, my admiration for Ages of the World
is equalled only by my admiration for Plato's
Parmenides. The uninitiated may well find this
catechism to be an ideal introduction to that
marvelous piece of poetry.

Nothing about Parmenides or Ages of the
World points to Chapter eight of this study. Yet
the inner logic of these two works (each of which
is written without the other in mind) stumble
unless there is something like Chapter eight as
a possible outcome. Those moves in the first
seven chapters which are consciously un-Schellingesque are made with a view toward the outcome
of Chapter eight.

John McGinley
University of Scranton
May 12, 1980

Table of Contents

Chapter One

THEOLOGY AS REVELATION

Q1. What is theology?

A1. Theology is the science OF God. Accordingly,
it can be looked upon as the science which has
God as its subject matter. In a more precise
sense, however, it is literally God's science.
It is the knowledge in God's possession.

Q2. What is the knowledge in God's possession?

A2. It is the separation of God from himself by
which God is and by which God is a self. This
separation is real and occurs in the mode of
eternity. This knowledge, then, is the eternal
differentiation of God from His own nature and
as such is, simultaneously, both condition for
and realization of the revelation of God.

Q3. What is the revelation of God?

A3. The revelation of God is the appearance of
God by God, for God and to God.

1

Q4. What is revealed in revelation and to whom is
it revealed.

A4. God is revealed in revelation. Revelation is
already (in the mode of eternity) other than God
even as it is God in and by the revelation of God.
Revelation is to other than God which also means
that revelation is to itself. In other words,
the "to whom" of revelation comes into being with
revelation itself. Of course "comes into being"
can occur according to the mode of eternity or
according to the mode of serial succession.

Q5. Then is God revealed both to Himself and to
other than Himself?

A5. Yes. But let it be noted that the other than
God -- even at the moment of extreme alienation
-- is never quite bereft of God.

Q6. How does God reveal Himself from Himself?

A6. By the freest of free acts.

Q7. From what is God revealed?

A7. From His own Nature.
    God's nature is the dimension of God which
is, so to speak, eternally dark in itself. It
comes to submit to that which is free in God.
"Comes to submit" in this sense happens in the
mode of eternity which means that the dark in
and of God submits to the free in God without
there having been any time (eternal or otherwise)
when the dark in God had not already and from
eternity submitted to the free in God.

2

Chapter Two

GOD

Q1. What is God?

A1. God is the unity of the fourfold.

Q2. What is the fourfold?

A2. It is: the two opposing poles of God's nature
interacting (3) in their unresolved unity and
then submitting (4) to the free. This interacting
(3) and submitting (4) have a kind of priority
and posteriority about them according to the mode
of eternity. But there is no sequential priority
and posteriority about them. The submission of
the three to the free of God brings with it and
is the revelation of God. Revelation, we shall
see, occurs both according to the eternal mode as
well as according to the mode of serial succession.

Furthermore, God eternally achieves definition and selfhood by virtue of this victory/
submission. In terms of the eternal victory/
submission the what of God is the Who of God.

Q3. What are the two opposing poles in and of

God's nature?

A3. It is the eternal contradiction. It is the
grand source of all opposition. It is that without which there would be no movement, life, power
or anything at all. For it is a mistake of pre-
vious Theology (to be examined in Chapter Seven)
to suppose that the absolutely simple -- even
when conceived as pure act and functioning as
final cause -- can be the cause of motion, life
and power. Yet even now it can be mentioned
that noteworthy mistakes in the history of
Theology can only be made by those who are --
despite themselves, as it were, -- milors of
God.

The usual dualistic pairings ("good and
evil", for example) by which this primordial
contradiciton might come to be expressed are
quite inadequate for expressing this primordial
contradiction residing in and as the heart of
God. For the usual dualistic pairings (again,
"good and evil", for example) are such that each
one of the terms in a given pairing are derivative
from the interaction of the two opposing poles of
God's eternal nature. In this sense, any given
term of the usual dualistic pairings cannot reflect
either one of the two opposing poles of God's
primordial nature prior, so to speak, to the
interaction in unresolved unity of the two
opposing poles of God's primordial nature.

Nonetheless, if the above caution is kept in
mind, the following can be stated. In any of the
usual dualistic pairings each respective term of
the pairing tends to reflect, predominantly, one
opposing pole of God's primordial nature while the
other term tends to reflect, predominantly, the
other opposing pole of God's primordial nature.

Q4. Granted the above caution, is there one dualistic pairing by which this eternal primordial
contradiciton -- which is God's primordial nature

4

-- is to be expressed?

A4. Yes. "The Yes and the No" expresses in a
most fundamental manner what this contradiction
is. The revelation of God is the expression of
God. "The Yes and the No" expresses and comes
to express what God is. ELOHIM and YAHWEH.

Q5. If contradiction is intrinsic to God's nature
-- if, indeed, contradiction is the eternal
primordial nature of God -- then there cannot be
any simplicity or unity about God.

A5. Not necessarily.
    There is a simplicity eternally residing in
God which is utterly simple. This simplicity
belongs to and basically is what must be called
the Godhead of God. The Godhead of God is the
ultimate source in terms of which God is God.
Yet the Godhead of God is not God. Further, it
is the Godhead of God -- and thus, not God, --
which is sufficient unto itself.

Q6. What is the Godhead of God?

A6. It is the free.

Q7. And what about the unity of God?

A7. The unity of God is said in several senses.
    In the first place there is the unified whole
which is God. This is: the two opposing poles
of God's primordial nature interacting in their
unresolved unity and then -- according to the
mode of eternity -- submitting to the free.

    In the second place, there is the unity of
the primordial contradiction. The eternal interaction of the two opposing poles of God's prim-

5

ordial nature is itself a unity although it
remains a unity which is unrevealed except by
virtue of submitting to the free. There is, then,
a kind of triunity in and of God's eternal nature:
the two contradictory poles of that nature and
their unity of eternal interaction.

In the third place, there is the utter unity
and simplicity of the Godhead itself which is
the free. The interactive unity of God's primordial nature becomes -- according to the mode of
eternity -- by submitting to the free. The
Godhead becomes God -- according to the mode of
eternity -- by virtue of its eternal victory over
God's primordial nature. The revelation of God
--according to the mode of eternity and also the
mode of serial succession -- occurs by virtue of
this union of the free and the other-than-the-
free. This other-than-the-free is the eternal
opposition of the two poles of God in their contradictory unity.

6

Chapter Three

THE FREE

Q1. What is the free?

A1. It is, negatively, that which and "in" which
there is no contraining contradiction whatsoever.
It is utter simplicity. It is quietness and
peace which eternally pre-exists (so to speak)
that which is. But as quietness and peace
(serenity) it is not at all that which (eternally
or otherwise) has undergone cessation from conflict.

It is perfect stillness which has never
become still. It is stillness in a pure and full
sense rather than the stillness which would result
from a condition of maximum entropy.

The free is, by itself, without being or becoming in either of the modes of eternity or
serial succession. The free, by itself, cannot
be expressed as any kind of relationship — not
even relationship to itself. There is no determination about the free, not even the self-contained determinacy of thought thinking itself.

The free is the Godhead of God and the
Godhead, by itself, has no need for the primordial
nature of God.

The free cannot be uttered for itterance is
in no way about it. Further, even in its relation-

ship (which comes to be) with the primordial
nature of God, the free is <u>utterer</u> while the
primordial nature of God is <u>the uttered</u>. But in
themselves and by themselves, so to speak, neither
the primordial nature of God nor the Godhead are
either utterer and/or uttered.

The free has no tension or conflict about it.
From it, by itself, nothing can or does emmanate.
As perfectly free and utterly undetermined it is,
in the magnificant words of Schelling, pure will.
It is the will which does not will.

Q3. Then according to what general term are we
to understand urges, desires and drives? Or,
better yet, what is will if in its purity it
represents no urges, drives or desires?

A3. In the contradictory and primordial nature
of God it is proper to speak only of a fundamental inward-turning urge (No) and the equally
findamental outward-turning urge (Yes) as well as
their equally fundamental unresolved unity. Urge
and counter urge in the primordial nature of God
are undefined (except in terms of each other),
not directed towards and end and, essentially
chaotic.

That which we refer to as passions, drives,
desires and appetites are defined in terms of a
network of particular and ultimate ends. In
contrast, any kind of positive goal or end --
either intrinsic or extrinsic -- is lacking in
the primordial nature of God. The primordial
nature of God requires something other than
itself in order for end-directed behaviour
(eternal or otherwise) to emerge, if it is to
emerge at all. This other is the free.

The free, in turn, as the will which does not
will, is not behaviour at all and certainly not
end-directed behaviour. Nor does the free have
any need for end-directed behaviour. Nonetheless,

8

end-directed behaviour emerges (eternally) from
the submission of the primordial nature of God
to the will which does not will.

It is the revelation of God which emerges
from this submission of the primordial nature of
God to the Godhead. It is in and through and by
revelation -- part of which is the creation of
God -- that desire (both eternal and temporal in
the sense of serial succession) and all the
derivatives of desire come to be. This "coming
to be" is, again and of course, both in the
eternal mode and in the mode of serial succession.
It is desire, along with all of its derivatives,
which is end directed.

As mentioned, the revelation of God "comes to
be" only by virtue of the submission of the
primordial nature of God to the Godhead, which
submission is the victory of the free over the
other-than-the-free. This submission -- which
is a relationship -- constitutes the eternal and
truly voluntary. It is this eternal and truly
voluntary which is referred to when one properly
speaks about the will of God. The Will of God
emerges from the submission of the primordial
nature of God to the will which does not will.
But the Will of God is not identical to the Will
which does not will. The Will of God is end-
directed even though God is His own end with
respect to Himself.

As previously mentioned, this submission of
the primordial nature of God to the Godhead is
at once the defining differentiation of God by
which God knows Himself. This knowledge is from
God and of God and has God as its end. The truly
voluntary is this knowledge. The eternal act of
desire which is the revelation of God is defined
in terms of knowledge and is knowledge.

Furthermore, all derivatives of desire in
creation (which, as will be seen, is the disintegrating externalization of God) are properly
defined in terms of knowledge. Even in creation

9

the truly voluntary cannot occur without knowledge. End directed behavious can and does occur
under conditions of partial ignorance, but as such
it is not truly voluntary, A corollary of this
-- for Ethics -- is that choices are not truly
voluntary since a degree of ignorance (at least
with regard to the outcome of behaviour) is the
pre-condition of choice. Indeed, it is only
through and by the free agency of choice that
certain outcomes come about at all. By definition, these outcomes cannot be known in advance.
It is one of the profundities of both Ethics and
Theology that choices are free without being
truly voluntary. [1]

Finally, the following can be noted. How
strange and paradoxical it would be -- but not
impossible -- if God Himself were to make some
choice not required of Him by His voluntary
nature. By such a choice God would risk the very
being of His eternally accomplished voluntary
nature by entering into the domain of ignorance.
What could possibly motivate such a suicidal
risk on the part of God?

Q4. Please summarize these distinctions you have
just made relative to the question of will and
Will in God.

A4. In the first place, there is pure timeless
freedom which is the will which does not will
and which is undetermined and undeterminable.
It is actively (so to speak) undetermined.

In the second place, and from eternity, there
is the chaotic in itself urge (inward turning)
and counter-urge (outward turning) and their
unresolved unity in the primordial nature of God.

In the third place, there is the eternal
emergence and eternal accomplishment of the
truly voluntary. The truly voluntary eternally
emerges as the primordial nature of God, submits

to the free which is the eternal victory of the
free over the other-than-the-free. This submission to the free is simultaneously the eternal
revelation of God -- namely, God's knowledge.
Thus the character of the truly voluntary is
knowledge.

In the further revelation of God occurring
in the mode of temporal succession there are
innumerable end-directed urges, drives, passions,
appetites, desires, and choices. They are what
they are and deserve their appropriate treatment
in some Anthropology, Cosmology, and Ethics.
But all urges, drives, passions, appetites, and
desires are truly voluntary if and only if they
occur with knowledge in such a way that knowledge
is the determining factor of their outcome. [2]

Q5. What is it about the primordial nature of God
which brings about its submission to the free?

A5. The need for this submission arises totally
from the primordial nature of God since the free,
as free, has no need about it at all. Thus the
initiative for this submission is from the primordial nature of God and not from the Godhead of
God.

There is in the primordial nature of God that
which is eternally dreadful, terrible, aw-full
and, as such, unendurable. It needs. It wants.
It withdraws. It goes out. All to no avail. It
is caught in -- and indeed is -- the eternal
unendurable cycle of urge and counter-urge. In
a thoughtless pre-determined manner it seeks out
submission to other.

As this submission eternally plays itself
out, the primordial nature of God orders its
triadic nature so that it may act as most appropriate ground (hupokeimenon) for the free as it
submits to the free. The No in itself submits
to the Yes in itself which submits to the Yes-and

11

-No in itself. It brings about a kind of triune harmony of itself. Thus its submission to the free as ground (hupokeimenon) of the free is such that it arranges itself for the best. With the imposition of freedom on itself God achieves a kind of eternal Self-Control with all of His "parts" arranged for the best. A kind of eternal fittingness is eternally achieved.

The free, groundless and needless in itself, becomes, according to the mode of eternity, grounded in the primordial nature of God. There is not ground (reason -- aitia) -- from the side of the free -- for the imposition of itself on the primordial nature of God. There is no "why" for God in this sense. God, considered from the side of the Godhead, has more the character of the "why not?" But the Godhead pays a price for the frivolous victory as will be shown.

In any case, both the primordial nature of God and the Godhead of God -- from differing directions as it were -- are what they are in this submission/victory. This is the stark and glorious givenness of God. It is this instant (eksaiphnes) that Revelation occurs. Of course the instant of this submission/victory never began to be even as it never ceases to begin to be. Revelation, then, is the posterior separation of God from Himself. Revelation is that eternal posterior differentiation of God from Himself by which the "parts" of God are, eternally for the first time defined. On the other hand, that anterior separation of the Godhead of God from the primordial nature of God -- prior to the submission/victory -- has no knowledge about it.

12

Notes

[1] Please cf. my more detailed discussion of these matters dealing with the Psychology of Moral Behaviour which occurs in Chapter Eight.

I have also discussed these matters by way of a critique of the Psychology of Moral Behaviour given by Aristotle in Nichomachean Ethics. My remarks are contained in "Aristotle's Notion of the Voluntary" which will be published in 1981 in the Australian journal, Apeiron.

[2] Cf. Note #1.

Chapter Four

ETERNITY

Q1. What is eternity?

A1. There are many meanings of eternity. Furthermore, the vocabulary of the eternal in any given
language -- along with the etymologies of the
various words employed -- gives a hint about the
complexities which are often covered over by the
all too facile assumptions which are normally
made about the most fundamental words. Still,
let us make a beginning.

In the tightest and strictest sense of eternity, eternity is the free. This is that
underived, perfect, undetermined and undeterminable stillness which "never" has become still.
In this sense, the eternal is timeless. It is
not even the eternal now since the eternal now,
as we shall see, is a mode of (eternal) time.

The Godhead, by itself, has no determination
whatsoever, not even the determination of "is"
or of "is not". To have any determination at all
is to be in time, as Plato made perfectly clear
long ago in Parmenides. 3 Even the perfect act
of being by which God (not the Godhead) is, is an
act of being which has (eternal) time about it in
some sense.

Yet, everything which comes to be --

including the eternal coming to be of God himself
-- is what it is by virtue of relationship to or
connection with the Godhead. Thus, if only in
some derived sense, the mark of the pure eternal
is on everything. Accordingly, there are derivative notions of eternity.

Q2. What are these derivative notions of eternity?

A2. In the first place, there are the three
eternities eternally spawned as the triadic
primordial nature of God eternally and hierarchically submits to the free. There is in God,
then, the eternal past, eternally submitted to
the eternal now which is eternally to be submitted
to the eternal outcome. All of these eternities
are spawned from their submission to the pure
timeless eternity of the Godhead "in" which, when
it is taken by itself, there is no time whatsoever
not even the perfection of the eternal now. The
fourfold character of eternity is clear.

In this sense, God is the eternal master of
his own household being an eternal act of Self-
Control in which the lower submits to the higher
in a relationship which is best for each of the
"parts" precisely because it is best for the
whole. As eternal Self-Control, God is the
fitting. This is the primordial character of
Justice.

The Justice of God, however, has the following curiosity about it. The whole of God is
ordered for the best by the submission of the
primordial nature of God to the Godhead of God.
The Godhead, in its gratuitous vistory over the
primordial nature of God, gains being and
revelation of its being in this victory. But as
perfectly free and undetermined, it is a "gain"
for which the Godhead, as Godhead, has no need.
On the other hand, the Godhead becomes compromised and partially determined in this victory/
submission. Thus, in a manner of speaking, the

16

Godhead of God is a kind of sacrificial victim
in its very freedom for the sake of the Justice
of God which is the good of the whole.

Q3. Are there further dimensions of eternity?

A3. Yes.

God, as the eternal submission of its primordial nature to the Godhead of God, is eternal
revelation. Revelation is God's knowledge by
and in which God is eternally differentiated
from His primordial nature. Of course, this
eternal differentiation is eternally posterior
to the primeval coming together of the free and
the primordial nature of God. The primordial
nature of God "now" rests in hierarchial order,
although it is hardly tamed or domesticated.

This eternal differentiation is itself
motivated and spawned by the interaction of God's
"Yes and No" as it, the interaction, submits to
the Godhead of God. This interaction of the "Yes
and the No" in its submission to the free is
grounded in the Yes of God's primordial nature
which in turn is grounded in the dark, inward
turning, of God's primordial nature. As such,
the whole requires an intricate scenario of
revelation. Revelation is precisely this defining
differentiation of these eternal dimensions of
God's being. This eternal (and posterior)
differentiation of God from Himself has the
character of self-knowledge.

The eternal character of knowledge (which, as
such, is also the truly voluntary) is not identical with the timeless Godhead. But in that
defining differentiation of God from himself,
the "godly part" of God, so to speak, returns, in
a mimicing fashion to the timlessness of the
Godhead "prior" to its eternal victory (viz.,
interaction with) the primordial nature of God.
This eternal character of knowledge (which is

17

simultaneously the truly voluntary) is, accordingly, best described as an eternal now rather than
as timelessness.

In this eternal now, God enjoys a self-sufficiency and finality, This godly aspect of God
can "thereafter" be threatened only by himself.
Only by choice (which is free, but not truly
voluntary) would God risk this godly aspect of
His being. Otherwise, this godly aspect of God,
in its (posterior) mimicing return to the Godhead
of God, remains self-contained in His own self-
knowledge and self-desire.

Q4. What else?

A4. The defining differentiation of God from
Himself, by which the godly "part" of God eternally
emerges, also brings the definition by which the
"ungodly" aspect of God emerges. In this differentiation, the ungodly of God returns, in a
mimicing fashion, to the primordial nature of God
"prior" to its submission to the Godhead. As
such, the ungodly aspect of God begins (i.e.,
eternally -- without ever having begun to begin)
to mimic its unrelieved state of internal contradiction.

However, the movement this time is away from
the Godhead, which alone can bring relief to the
primordial nature of God. Explosive disintegration is the resolution of eternal contradiction
as it moves (posteriorly) away from the godly
aspect of God and, so to speak, turns itself
inside out from the very heart of primordial pain,
dread and anguish. This is the eternal generation
(which never began to be generated since it is
ceaselessly generated) of space. Space, in
itself so to speak, is the chaotic shimmering
which has the character of being the receptacle
relative to that which is other than itself.

18

Q5. And?

A5. At the point of maximum separation from His
ungodly aspect, God eternally achieves the perspective which allows for the eternal glimpses
of all that can be as the godly aspect of God
(viz., Self-Knowledge and Self-Desire according
to the mode of eternity) returns to the now
alienated (othered) ungodly aspect of God.

Q6. Two questions: what are these glimpses and
what motivates the return of the godly aspect of
God to the ungodly aspect of God?

A6. These glimpses are the seeing-seen as the
truly voluntary makes its eternal return, posteriorly, to its own primordial (but now alienated)
nature. They are the models-to-be-made-actual-in
-variated-multiplicity through the return to God's
primordial (but now alienated) nature. They are
reflections from the future-becoming-past appear-
ing in the mind of God as God longingly looks
toward the shimmering chaos now alienated from
the godly aspect of God.

Q7. Why "longingly"? In general, what motivates
the return of the godly aspect of God -- self-
sufficient in its own Self-knowledge and Self-
desire -- to the ungodly and alienated aspect of
God?

A7. Sweet bittersweet eros which always seeks
wholeness. Divine eros as it travels downward
in its circular journey. Natural and human eros
as it travels upward in its circular journey.
But even today -- with all of our hermeneutical
sophistication -- the Symposium largely remains
translated but un-read.

This return is basically the non-jealousy of
God related to us by Plato in Timaeus. It is

compatible with the self-motivated and self-contained desire of God's differentiated nature. This return on the part of the godly of God to the ungodly of God is simply a natural tendency -- often noted by practically all theologians -- to communicate goodness. The return to His alienated primordial nature is a free act of God which stays within the truly voluntary dimension of God's posterior being. God knows from eternity the flawed manner in which the alienated "part" of God is redeemed by this return. Yet from the eternal perspective, some redemption is better than none. Is the glass half full or half empty?

Q8. Must the redemptive return to the alienated nature of God necessarily be flawed?

A8. Yes and No.

With the explosive disintegration and externalization of itself the alienated nature of God falls outside of the Divine circle of self-knowledge and self-desire. God can "overflow" to His alienated nature. But this "overflow" cannot by itself bring His alienated back into the Divine circle of self-knowledge and self-desire. Further movement from God and from God's alienated nature as well would be required to bring God's alienated nature back into the Divine circle of self-knowledge and self-desire. By definition, however, further movement on the part of God would take God into the domain of ignorance with regard to outcome. Such further movement would, by definition, risk the collapse of God's truly voluntary nature. Yet who knows for sure what God would or would not do to bring back His alienated nature to the circle of Divine self-knowledge and self-desire?

Q9. With all of this about "glimpses", space, chaos, the receptacle and alienation, has our

Catechism now become nothing more than a likely story?

A9. Nothing is wrong with a likely story when it is fabricated by a thinker in tune with God. In any case, any serious investigation -- be it as dry and un-storylike as possible -- about the Divine life will have about it the atmosphere suggested by these words from Schelling:

What holds back the anticipated golden age when truth again becomes fable and fable truth? 4

Theology is far and away the most fabulous of the sciences.

Q10. And?

A10. With the eternal glimpses eternally attained, the eternal posterior return to the now alienated primordial nature of God begins -- in the mode of eternity. At this stage God forms from chaos -- just as chaos itself experiences the first stirrings of a longing for the godly aspect of God -- those perspectives which allow for the various moving images of eternity. As images, there is a degree of deception in them. Yet they are useful illusions allowing for a partial return of the alienated nature of God to the godly aspect of God.

Some of these moving images of eternity involve the stars formed from that about chaos which is most visible. Some of these moving images of eternity are "psychological" in nature implanted in souls which are partly formed from the Divine overflow and partly formed from the less visible dimension of chaos.

In any case, these moving images of eternity are there to awaken -- when the time and conditions are right -- the memory of eternity and the

21

Godhead which is posteriorly present in the primordial nature of God, even and precisely as
alienated. In this fashion the alienated nature
of God gives rise -- according to the mode of
serial succession -- to the No, the Yes, and the
Yes-and-No of God's nature which is still present
in it. Thus is accomplished even in alienation
the temporal mirror of God by which the play of
revelation is further manifested.

Q11. Is this play the Divine Comedy or the
Divine Tragedy?

A11. Both. Its denouement requires insight from
special revelation. For now, further classifica-
tions.

Notes

[3]I am referring, of course, to the "time" section
of hypothesis #2 of Plato's dialogue Parmenides.
I have a printed but unpublished discussion of
that dialogue -- indeed a detailed commentary
--if further reference is required.

[4]Cited from Friedrich Schelling's Ages of the
World; translation and introduction by Frederick
De Wolf Bolman; AMS Press, Inc., 1967. Page 84.
Hereafter: Ages.

Chapter Five

THE SEXUALITY OF GOD

Q1. Is there sexuality in God?

A1. Sexuality is, perhaps, the perfect image for what God is.

Q2. In what manner is sexuality, perhaps, the most perfect image for what God is?

A2. In several manners.

In the first place, sexuality is differentiation within the same (species) for the sake of continuing (**revealing**) the same (species).

In the second place, **sexuality is the** intense longing for a **re-union** to that which, arising from the same, is now other and alienated.

In the third place, it is in the human species that sexuality takes on its most intense and variated forms.

Q3. Why should the human instantiation of sexuality be of such import to these theological investigations, even if sexuality in general is an accurate image of what God is?

A3. In response to that question, one must cite Schelling again:

Everything divine is human, and everything human divine. 5

What this citation does or does not imply with regard to the transcendency of God will be discussed later. For now let us use it as the key for unlocking the secrets of God.

With regard to sexuality as an image for revealing the nature of God, this statement by Schelling will mean the following. Only with the human species is the nature of sexual differentiation so intimately connected with the grand questions of knowledge, voluntary behaviour and the penalty of death. This concatenation of sex, knowledge and the possibility of choice was caught most efficiently in Chapters Two and Three of Genesis. It is precisely this concatenation which reveals for us the structure of God.

Q4. Is God, then, male or female?

A4. The dualistic pairing, "male and female", is a most interesting reflection -- albeit derivative and in creation -- of the two dualities in and of God.

In the primordial contradictory nature of God there is incessant (inward-turning) urge/(outward-turning) counter-urge and their unresolved unity. If the sexuality of God is properly located in the primordial nature of God, then God is both female and male and the unresolved unity of the two. Still, as mentioned earlier, no derived dualistic pairing occurring in creation can quite catch or express God's primordial contradictory nature. For derived dualistic pairings represent posterior differentiations from interaction and not the primordial contradiction eternally giving rise to interaction.

26

The sexuality of God, however, is most clearly
manifested in the submission of the primordial
nature of God to the Godhead of God. In this
submission -- unconsciously initiated by the
primordial nature of God -- all in the primordial
nature of God comes to be hierarchically ordered
for the best. In its gratuitous imposition of
itself on God's primordial nature of the Godhead
of God sets loose the process of God's revelation
of Himself. The analogue for this would be the
offspring resulting from the sexual union of male
and female.

Q5. Is God best described as androgynous?

A5. The true dimensions of the androgynicity of
God are revealed only to the extent that male and
female are set off and distinguished one from
another in their essential difference. If the
essential difference between male and female is
not brought into sharp focus, then mere formula-
tions expressing the androgynicity of God are
without significance.

Furthermore, if the clear and sharp distinction between male and female is clouded over in
a frenzy of egalitarian thoughtlessness, then
the intense androgynous drama of each individual
male and of each individual female is likely to
disappear. To that extent our ability to become
and be mirrors of God is hopelessly diminished.

We humans, male and female alike, are made in
the androgynous image of an androgynous God.
True androgynicity requires -- both in thought
and in life -- the sharp distinction between
male and female as its condition of possibility.
When this sharp distinction is lost then the very
drama of life is lost.

Q6. If God is androgynous, why is the pronoun "he" used to speak of God?

A6. It is, by the metaphor taken from male and female in creation, the female in and of God which submits to the male in and of God. God is at all and is what He is by virtue of this submission of female -- unconsciously initiated by the female of God -- to male. It is the male in God which enjoys this gratuitous victory over the female in God. As noted earlier and as to be explained later, the Godhead of God pays a penalty for this unsolicited victory which points to a kind of unfairness eternally present in the Justice of God. In any case, starting from the metaphor of male and female taken from male and female in creation, it is totally fitting that God be called "He" since it is the male of God which dominates.

Of course in the posterior alienation of the primordial nature of God -- (viz., the female of God "now" containing something of the Godhead of God) -- from the posterior self-contained knowledge of God, it is the female of and in God which disintegrates into that shimmering receptacle by which it is the mother and nurse of the generated cosmos.

Thus it is the whole androgynous drama which, in image fashion, is to be played out in each human male and in each human female. Genetic biology is but stage setting (imposing some intractable limitations) for the playing out of the grand androgynous drama. In this fashion it is the female of each male which should -- if the imitation of God is to be successful -- submit to the male of each male. Likewise, it is the female of each female which should -- if the imitation of God is to be successful -- submit to the male of each female.

Finally, it is to be noted, the long journey of those souls destined to take on human form always involves time spent in both male and female

28

form. All souls are first incarnated -- (and not all at the same time) -- as human males. When all souls in their long journeys will have taken on female form, then the end of time will be at hand. But the time of this time cannot be known with certitude according to this measure. For there are no females who have not first been males; but there may still be souls, presently incarnated as males, who have not yet taken on female form.

Notes

[5]Ages of the World, p. 179.

Chapter Six

MODES OF REVELATION

Q1. What are the modes of Revelation?
A1. There is general revelation which is primary
and there is special revelation.

Q2. What is the difference between general
revelation and special revelation?
A2. In a basic sense there is no difference.

There is nothing in special revelation which
is not already contained -- as discoverable
without special revelation -- as an actuality
or possibility of general revelation. Furthermore, they have this in common. Each of them
separately, and each of them in their relationship
to each other, are capable of misunderstanding
and misappropriation. Both, more often than not,
have been misunderstood and misappropriated.

They supplement and support each other
although there is nothing in the one which is
not also -- at least implicitly as a possibility
-- in the other. They together constitute God's
grand duet with Himself, by Himself, and for
Himself. For God is the subject matter of both
special and general revelation. We who write
words like these and you who read them are a bit

31

like musical instruments -- which can come to be
out of tune -- played by God.

There is, however, this difference.

General revelation, of its intrinsic nature
and not only by virtue of human weakness, is a
failure. Sometimes a comic failure; sometimes
a most tragic failure. But necessarily a failure.
Furthermore, general revelation is a continuing
failure which neither could be avoided not is it
to be avoided by human choice alone.

Special revelation, in contrast, is the
gamble for success. As such it need not be
understood, appreciated or sympathized with along
the way. It need not justify itself according
to the ephemeral even as it makes its way, pain-
stakingly, through the ephemeral. More often than
not it is either unnoticed and, when noticed,
misunderstood, misappropriated, and scorned. Yet
its justification is in terms of outcome. There
is no greater honor for a human than to be a part
of special revelation.

Chapter Seven

GENERAL REVELATION

Q1. What is general revelation?

A1. In the first place, general revelation is that
eternal (and posterior) differentiation of the
godly aspect of God from His ungodly aspect by
which God, as the godly aspect of God, is, at
once, that eternal act of self-knowledge which,
as such, is the truly voluntary. In that posterior separation of God from Himself resides,
eternally, the alienation of God from Himself.
This alienated ungodly aspect of God painfully
-- from the very heart of disintegrating anguish
-- gives rise to (becomes) the shimmering chaos/
space which functions as the mother and nurse of
all becoming and temporal coming into being
according to the mode of serial succession. This
painful externalization of God from Himself sets
the stage for the grand posterior return of God to
His alienated Self in the attempt to mAximize,
in accordance with the godly aspect of God, and
spread to the limit the revelation of Himself.

Q2. Whence the motivation for revelation at all?

A2. The prior union of the free with the primordial nature of God -- which union is God -- is
already a revelation. The two sides of God "now"
have an in-which, to-which, and by-which they are.

33

To be at all requires this other in which. To
be at all is to reveal through the other.

This original base of revelation, then, dupli-
cates itself by effecting from eternity that
differentiation from itself by which the ungodly
of God and the godly of God are defined. Yet in
this duplication for the sake of revelation an
ironic twist comes to pass. In that defining
differentiation by which God is what He is, God
loses himself in two ways.

In the first place, the Godhead of God (which
priorly gains the gratuitous victory over the
primordial nature of God) is compromised in its
victory. For in that eternal posterior differentiation the Godhead of God, eternally, is "in
part" held hostage by and in the alienated ungodly
aspect of God.

In the second place, in its alienation from
the   godly aspect of God, the ungodly aspect of
God suffers disintegration and externalization.
In this sense, the ungodly of God is not only
other from the godly aspect of God but is, so to
speak, further "othered" from the godly aspect
of God by becoming other from itself. Accordingly,
this othered other, by which and through which
there is revelation, must be brought back to
itself to the extent that it is possible. And all
of this, in the now partially ironic sense, for
the sake of revelation.

Q3. Is this a doctrine of pantheism?

A3. In some ways, yes. Essentially, however,
there is no pantheism in this teaching.

Shimmering chaos -- which turns out to be, in
effect, the raw material of all becoming and
temporal coming into being according to the mode
of serial succession -- is the externalization
(resulting from disintegration) of the ungodly

34

aspect of God at the eternal point of God's
extreme alienation from Himself. This ungodly
aspect of God "now" (viz., from eternity) includes
something of the Godhead about it since the separation referred to here is eternally "after" the
original submission of the primordial nature of
God to the Godhead. In this eternal victory/
submission -- (viz., nothing other than the
eternal trick) -- the Godhead is compromised, for
it is "now" gratuitously grounded (viz., is) in
other than itself. Likewise, something of the
primordial nature of God comes to be in the "now"
compromised Godhead. This continuing presence
in the other, along with the other's continuing
presence in it, is the eternal price paid by the
Godhead for its gratuitous victory over the
primordial nature of God.

In any case, all of this implies that something of the Godhead is held hostage, so to speak,
in and by the ungodly aspect of God even as,
through that defining differentiation, the one
side of God posteriorly mimics the prior purity
of the Godhead while the other side of God posteriorly mimics its prior primordial nature. In
this alienation from Himself, the ungodly aspect
of God ("now" with something of the Godhead in it
as hostage) disintegrates and externalizes itself.
Thus, something of God -- inclusive of the Godhead
-- is present in and is the mother and nurse of
all becoming and serial temporal succession.
Should this be called pantheism?

Not really.

Recall that in the disintegrating externalization of itself the ungodly aspect of God ("now"
inclusive of something of the Godhead) becomes
other than itself precisely by virtue of its
disintegration/externalization.

Recall also that in God's alienation from
Himself, God as knowledge and the truly voluntary
in no way disintegrates or externalizes Himself.
On this level especially God remains totally,

utterly and completely other -- although other
from Himself. Can a teaching which retains the
otherness of God on every level be called a
pantheism? Beware of the traps which come when
words and labels are used thoughtlessly.

Q4. How does general revelation proceed?

A4. Historically, and in such a manner that the
eternal No, the eternal Yes, and the eternal
Yes-and-No of God will come to be revealed in
that hierarchical arrangement.

In this sense, history is first of all eternal,
recording from eternity the eternal coming to be
of God arising from the eternal past of God which
eternally results in the eternal now of God.
Only in a derivative sense is history the recording of sequential events.

Furthermore, history eternally begins --
without there ever being a beginning -- as the
history of the cosmos. Each stage in cosmic
history becomes more definite as the impression
of the truly voluntary -- by way of its non-
jealous overflow -- in the shimmering receptacle
brings more definition. From the side of
shimmering chaos serial succession begins as it
responds from its side to the overtures from the
godly aspect of God. For precisely as disintegrated externalization the alienated nature of
God ("now" inclusive to some degree of the Godhead
to God) suffers a nostalgia for that from which
it is alienated. No matter that -- by the norms
of general revelation -- the rupture cannot be
fully repaired. The universe is alive by virtue
of this nostalgia -- alive in a condition of
blissful ignorance.

Human history is but a derivative from cosmic
history. However the temporal priority of cosmic
history (called "prehistory" by the historians)
is not priority with regard to the measure of

36

revelation which comes to be revealed through it.
It is only with the flourishing of the mirror of
God that revelation itself comes to flourish in
the order of serial succession.

Everything divine is human and
everything human divine. 6

Q5. What is the mirror of God?

A5. God and the Cosmos, of course. But in the
order of serial succession it is mankind --
individually and collectively -- which is the
mirror of God most especially.

Mirrors can be rusty, poorly made, deceptive,
dirty, adequate or inadequate. Mirrors can also
truly reflect. Mirrors can reflect each other
and thereby reflect that, other than a mirror,
which is to be reflected. Mirrors can reflect
each other and thereby fail to reflect that which
is to be reflected.

Q6. How does man become the mirror of God?

A6. By the union of male and female. By knowledge.
By living out the penalty of death. By compromise.
By failed attempts at grandeur. By success. By
shame and guilt. By shitting and keeping it neat.
By art, poetry, music, and dance. By war. By
peace. By love and hate. By prayer and silence.
By tragedy and comedy. Through pleasure and pain.
By freedom. By freedom played out without the
benefit of knowledge. By choice in the midst of
moral dilemma. By disintegration and recovery.
By self-control. By courage in the face of
difficulty. By jealousy and outrage. By love
and affirmation. By closing in upon oneself. By
meditation and self-knowledge. By Philosophy.

Q7. By Philosophy? What is that?

A7. An epiphenomenon of human history. A mirror off in the corner. Throughout most of its history it is an embarrassment, especially for those who understood its potential. Failure is the common thread running throughout human history; but in Philosophy failure is of the essence. One literally cringes in embarrassment when one measures the egoism, self-deception, and false grandeur characteristic of Philosophy and the so-called philosophers. And yet ...

Q8. And yet what?

A8. And yet Philosophy is the mirror most fitting for the expression of the general revelation of God. For Philosophy itself -- (you will discover if you study its history) -- is always born in the kind of alienation which has gone sour. This experience (pathein) is the pre-requisite for those who would reflect and thereby reveal God.

All Philosophy is a kind of fabrication. But sometimes the fabrication finds itself in tune with the original Fabricator. Then pure radiance shines forth from Philosophy.

Still, by and large, Philosophy is but a puerile embarrassment. One can learn more from the speech of Callicles in Georgias than from the vast majority of philosophers. Even so, from the very worst from its pantheon of heroes (from Hegel, for example) one can learn much that is positive if one has the time to wade through the garbage. Indeed, some tolerance for that which is all too human in Philosophy is required so that the positive from this embarrassing history can be rescued. After a while one becomes skilled in discerning the true and rare gems in this comedy of errors.

38

Q9. Are there not some in the history of philosophy who claim to be at least partially inspired by what you are calling "special revelation"?

A9. It was totally to be expected that -- (over the course of human history) -- those mirrors most disposed, despite their respective egoism, to be the mirrors of God would come to have some affinity for the light made possible through special revelation.

But several cautions are in order here.

In the first place, the history of special revelation was itself mired in much misunderstanding and misappropriation. The nature and function of special revelation will be studies in the next chapter along with a brief outline of its misappropriation.

In the second place, the following can be noted. Generally, the use by philosophers and thinkers (e.g., Kierkegaard) of special revelation has been a variated misuse of special revelation. In most cases, this misuse of special revelation has been superimposed upon a prior and institutionalized misappropriation of special revelation. Thus even the very terms which these philosophers and thinkers use to talk about the multi-faceted relationship between philosophy and special revelation both skews and falsifies both philosophy and special revelation and, most especially, the multi-faceted relationship which can obtain between philosophy and special revelation.

In the third place, however, it must be noted that thinkers can be stimulated in a positive fashion by that which they do not understand and even by that which they abuse. So thinkers such as St. Thomas Aquinas and Blaise Pascal -- to mention two of the greats -- became grand mirrors of God even as (precisely because?) they misunderstood the nature, function, and content of special revelation.

Q10. Where and how does Philosophy catch the No of God?

A10. Philosophy has almost never caught the dark No of God which is the prius, so to speak, of the primordial nature of God. What is dark-appearing about God Philosophy usually ascribes to the inability of human intellect to comprehend the Divine being. But there is a darkness in and of God quite aside from any difficulty which arises from the limitations of human intellect. For the most part, Philosophy shies away from even recognizing this intrinsic darkness in and of God.

Divine Plato, however, seems to have had some intimations about the dark-in-itself side of God's nature. In Timaeus he speaks of the intractability of "necessity" with which reason, as demiurge, must compromise. Likewise, in hypothesis number five of his theological work, Parmenides he exhibits an exact fascination for this most strange "thing", namely, the one-which-is-not.

Unfortunately, both the Timaeus and the Parmenides have wrongly been held hostage by a tradition which, least of all, has understood the dark side of God. This is the tradition of Plotinus and Christian Neo-Platonis, which can only understand the darkness of God as a function of the inability of finite intellect to comprehend utter transcendence as though the transcendence of God were merely a function of His "beyond". Neo-Platonism bypasses totally what is essentially dark about God precisely in the so-called mystical dimensions of Neo-Platonic thought. Since they hold Timaeus and Parmenides hostage to their false schema of things, the manner in which Plato was a theologian goes un-noticed in the history of Philosophy.

Q11. Where and how does Philosophy catch the Yes of God?

40

All. We have not finished with the No of God.

There is in God the No which emerges, eternally, when and as the primordial nature of God submits to the Godhead of God. This is the spawning of the eternal No. But this No, "now" (eternally) harmonized by its integration with the Godhead, is no longer dark and foreboding. This No is simply the eternal self-containment of God.

This No, which expresses both God's otherness from the world and His independence from the world is best caught by Aristotle in Book Twelve, Chapter Seven of Metaphysics. (hereafter: "XII-7") This is, of course, the analysis of God as pure act which has no potency about it. This conclusion leads Aristotle to the natural corollary that such a being is both absolutely simple and necessary. The necessity named by Aristotle in XII-7 is not at all the dark necessity of God named by Plato in Timaeus. Aristotle's necessity is but the expression for absolute simplicity which, having no potency about it, cannot be other than it is and therefore must be what it is. It is this Aristotelian notion of necessity which predominates in that portion of the history of Philosophy which concerns itself with the nature of God.

This No of God's otherness and self-containment is also caught, in an infantile fashion, by the various traditions -- both Plotinian and Christian -- of New-Platonism. This development in the history of Philosophy should be called "New-Aristotelianism" since it uses, (even when it is not conscious of its historical source), as its base the God developed by Aristotle in XII-7. Neo-Platonism takes this Aristotelian God and makes the object of a badly misconstrued "via negativa" Theology.

True "via negativa" Theology -- presumably practiced by Plato in Parmenides -- reveals what is negative and dark in and of God with subtle

41

precision. Neo-Platonism, having only the
Aristotelian God at its disposal, (which has no
negativity about it other than its otherness
from the world) locates the negative of "via
negativa" merely in the inadequacy of human
language as a vehicle for the expression of God.
But the true negativity of God is not even guessed
at by the simple-headed observation that human
intellect and human language are inadequate
vehicles for understanding and expressing "the
One". On the contrary, man, as the mirror of
God, is finite, inadequate and limited precisely
because of the dark and negative in and of God.

As infantile Aristotelians, the Neo-Platonists
deserve only minor condemnation -- and indeed some
celebration -- for the puerility of their "via
negativa" Theology. For after all, they, along
with Aristotle, do reveal the Divine otherness
and self-containment. But as barriers to the
true understanding of Plato they, even today,
impede the appreciation of the best map available
of what is dark and foreboding in and of God.

Q12. Where and how does Philosophy catch the Yes
of God?

A12. The Yes contained in the primordial nature of
God "prior" to its eternal submission to the
Godhead is caught in a flurry of minor thinkers
in the nineteenth and twentieth centuries.
Bergson, especially, comes to mind. But others
such as Whitehead and Scheler, come to mind as
well. They all take their essential insight and
try to make more of it than the insight deserves.
By forcing the other phenomena of the Divine life
to center around this Yes they falsify the nature
of God. They function as mirrors whose revealing
flash is immediately spattered with mud.

However, in a more accurate and sustained
manner, this Yes of God was caught in the Will
side of Schopenhaur's Philosophy. Will in

42

Schopenhaur is quite radically different from the
will-which-does-not-will formalized by Schelling.
Schelling's will-which-does-not-will is a formu-
lation for the Godhead of God. Schopenhaur's
Will refers to the eternal, affirmative, outward-
moving counter-urge darkly present in the primordial nature of God.

From the pain of Schopenhaur is birthed the
glory of Nietzsche who makes the Schopenhaurian
Will -- now jazzed up as the Will to Power --
into a kind of unitary, arrifming life force
characteristic of reality as a whole. Most of
what Nietzsche says about the Will to Power (and
its Nietzschean corollaries) is puerile to a
fault and is all too human. Nonetheless, before
the clouds of syphilitically induced madness
fall down over his consciousness, he took his
teaching of the Will to Power to the very gates
of eternity.

Because his base -- the doctrine of the Will
to Power -- is decisively insufficient, its
mixture with the genuine Nietzschean encounter
with eternity births only the old Pythagorean
(and then, Stoical) teaching of the Eternal
Recurrence of the Same.

The failure of Nietzsche is not at all that
his doctrines of the Will to Power and of the
Eternal Recurrence of the Same are incompatible.
On the contrary, a close reading of the last
section of The Will to Power shows how perfectly
compatible the two teachings are.

Rather, the failure of Nietzsche is that he
did not bring sufficient subtlety with him on
that walk on the mountain when he discovered
eternity. He (viz., his doctrine of the Will to
Power) did not know how to submit to freedom and
thus freedom slips away from the Nietzschean
system. With Nietzsche -- his words to the
contrary notwithstanding -- the pale ghost of
freedom haunts his system as it did for the
ancient Stoics and for the nihilistic calmness

43

of Buddhism. The fullness of A-PATHEIN; the
Eternal Recurrence of the Same. These are grand
doctrines. But they sadly fall short of the
Nietzschean promise.

Indeed the Nietzschean instincts cry out for
more than Nietzsche's grand thought -- the Eternal
Recurrence of the Same -- can deliver. Had he
more subtly prepared himself for his encounter
with eternity he would have come back from that
mountain walk mimicing Schelling. Interestingly
enough -- in a text whose authenticity is ques-
tioned by practically all Nietzsche scholars --
Nietzsche says the following:

> This is the fantastic paradox
> of life: we must dangle from the
> cross, crucified between two thieves
> of freedom and necessity, as Jesus
> is eternally crucified (Pascal) for
> the life of the spirit hinges on an
> agonizing contradiction that drives
> the sanest mind into madness! 7

Q13. Where and how does Philosophy catch the
Yes-and-No of God?

A13. We are not finished with the Yes of God.

The eternal Yes which is spawned when and as
the primordial nature of God submits to the Godhead is caught, for the first time, by divine
Plato. The non-jealous movement of Divine Reason
(as demiurge) to and into intractable Necessity
is the Yes of God. The circle of Divine desire,
so carefully orchestrated by Plato in Symposium,
is the expression of this eternal Yes of God.

Only a few know how to read the Symposium
whose sub-title is "concerning the good" and which
takes place at the home of the tragic playwright
names "good". The Philebus (which itself says
a few things about the good and which, as the

44

second dialogue of the third tetralogy introduces
the earlier-written Symposium which is the third
dialogue of the third tetralogy) says the following:

> If a man (from the context,
> "the good") had to be found, and
> you could discover in what house
> he lived, would not that be a
> great step towards the discovery
> of the man himself? [8]

If you would learn Plato's doctrine of the good,
go to the house of Agathon. There you will find
a tragic poet (maker) and a necessarily flawed
circle of desire.

A puerile attempt to catch the eternal Yes
of God is attempted by Plotinian and Christian
versions of New-Platonism through emmanation
theory. Philo, who was reasonably and accurately
enough in touch with special revelation, had
spawned the thinking which goes by the name of
emmanation theory. But that which is reasonably
spawned by Philo, given his theological milieu,
came to be perverted by Plotinus and his Christian
counter-parts.

The appropriation of emmanation theory
requires a positive understanding of the free in
God. Likewise, the appropriation of emmanation
theory requires a grasp of that other to which
emmanation is directed and without which there
could be no emmanation. Thus, the positive
understanding of the free in God requires a God
who, while remaining the simple, necessary and
self-contained being of XII-7, is, simultaneously,
both beyond and before such self-containment.

The Neo-Platonists, in contrast, (who,
precisely in their most allegedly mystical moments
of their falsely construed "via negativa" theology)
have only Aristotle's necessary being at their
disposal. They, accordingly, wrongfully enter
into emmanation theory. They have no positive

conception of the free in and of God. Likewise, the only "other" they know is of mere privation. They have no understanding of the essential, in itself, darkness which is the condition without which there is no meaning for emmanation theory. Neo-Platonism is precisely the wrong vehicle by which to understand, in a positive manner, the significance of emmanation theory.

Early Christian theologians -- including the author(s) of the fourth Gospel -- attempt to catch the eternal Yes of God. Then, and throughout the centuries, this attempt has led to exaggerated accounts of the so-called "agape" notions of love which allegedly inspired the first generation of Christian Jews. In point of fact, such "agape" notions of Divine love do catch something of the eternal Yes of God. But to catch the eternal Yes in God is but to catch an intrinsic -- but hardly exhaustive -- dimension of revelation. To focus in upon it to the exclusion of the other intrinsic dimensions of revelation is to be untrue to both special and general revelation.

A thoughtful attempt to catch the eternal Yes of God was attempted by St. Thomas Aquinas in those sections of Summa Theologica in which he explains the Will of God.

Working with the Aristotelian concept of God, St. Thomas -- especially in question Nineteen -- carefully shows that the other-directedness implied by the notion of there being a Will in God is compatible with the self-sufficiency of God demanded both by traditional Christian concepts of God and the Aristotelian base which he, St. Thomas, uses as raw material.

The stumbling block for St. Thomas is his understanding of how God is an absolutely simple being. For St. Thomas, God in His entire nature is an absolutely simple being. The simplicity of God can in fact be squared with the God of XII-7. But -- St. Thomas' attempt notwithstanding

46

-- the notion of an absolutely simple being is
incompatible with a God in which the God of XII-7
is superimposed on eternal self-desire (God's
will) which, eternally, is other (creation)
directed as well.

For Schelling, it is the Godhead of God
which alone is absolutely simple. The other dimensions of God, by submission to the Godhead,
gain a kind of derived simplicity. Not armed
with this subtlety, St. Thomas never quite catches
a clear expression of the will of God. Yet
submission to the discipline of St. Thomas is the
key by which Schelling can be approached.

Of course St. Thomas is of no value whatsoever
in his understanding of special revelation or of
the multi-faceted manner in which special revelation is and can be related to general revelation.
St. Thomas, no doubt, was subjectively inspired to
philosophical heights by virtue of his understanding of special revelation and of its multi-faceted
relationship to the life of the mind. But St.
Thomas is, in point of fact, a bright and steady
mirror of God despite -- not because of -- his
understanding of special revelation.

An orgasm of expressing the eternal Yes of
God is pushed through by Hegel, most especially
in the work called Phenomenology of Spirit. The
intricate way in which the absolute comes to be
"with us" is a journey the expression of which by
Hegel is not without its thoughtful moments.

It is Hegel who lends imagination to the
self-containment of Aristotle's God. God comes
to Himself through Himself. By giving Himself as
other than Himself God creates the medium by which
God comes to Himself. Hegel takes an imaginative
understanding of Christian trinitarian theology
and grafts it unto an imaginative understanding
of the God portrayed by Aristotle in XII-7.
Hegel is a kind of daring St. Thomas liberated
by the heady atmosphere prevailing during the
heyday of German Idealism.

But as with Nietzsche, the ghost of freedom haunts the Hegelian system. For Hegel, God, through the medium of Nature and Finite Spirit, is impelled by an inner necessity. The only freedom Hegel can recognize is the freedom already implied by Aristotle's Theology. The absolutely necessary being, since it is not determined by anything other than itself, is the absolutely free being. The implicit identity between necessity and freedom of Arostotle's Theology now becomes the explicit identity of necessity and freedom of Hegel's Theology.

In point of fact, this identity between freedom and necessity does characterize the eternal No of God resulting from the submission of the primordial nature of God to the Godhead. But neither the full character of the free nor the full character of the primordial nature of God are caught in the expression of the eternal No of God resulting from the submission of the primordial nature of God to the Godhead. Aristotle's valid conception of God given in XII-7 expresses a true dimension of God which is, however, ill suited for expressing the Yes of God.

If, nonetheless, an imaginative thinker, properly enamoured of XII-7 (as Hegel was) were to use this God concept for expressing the eternal Yes of God, then falsification sets in. Aristotle's God is compatible with the eternal Yes of God but is anything but the vehicle by which this eternal Yes is to be expressed.

The expression of the eternal Yes of God requires two things. A direct taste of the free Godhead of God is required. Also, a direct appreciation of the "prior" separation of the primordial Nature of God from the Godhead of God "before" its submission to the Godhead of God. These Hegel totally lacks.

The eogtistical desire to explain everything even if it is not understood, is epitomized in the person of Hegel. He will drive through and

48

have his orgasm even if the bride is not ready.
Despite its thoughtful moments, Hegel, even and
especially in the Phenomenology of Spirit, is
the symbol of a selfish and botched-up job.

It is Hegel, of course, who, from the heart
of cuteness, makes reference to the night in
which all cows are painted black. In one phrase
he acknowledges the influence of his teacher who
was five years his junior and allegedly super-
cedes him. Nonetheless, there may be more than
a little truth to the allegation that the
Phenomenology of Spirit was, in its essentials,
a straight out plagarism of Schelling's developing
"Philosophy of Identity". If this is so, then we
owe to Hegel an immense debt of gratitude. This
betrayal -- if it is such -- literally freed
Schelling for the quiet but meaningful glory
contained in Ages of the World.

Q14. Where and how does Philosophy express the
Yes-and-No of God in its unresolved unity?

A14. Perhaps in Heraclitus, the obscure one.

Perhaps in Nicholas of Cusa, although this
is doubtful since Christian Neo-Platonists
appear to be endemically allergic to encountering
the dark nature of God. Nonetheless. the Neo-
Platonism of Nicholas is of a different order from
the Neo-Platonism of Plotinus and his Christian
derivatives.

Q15. Where and how does Philosophy express the
unresolved unity of the unresolved Yes-and-No
of God as it eternally emerges from the submission
of the primordial nature of God to the Godhead of
God?

A15. Now we have come to the moment of subtlety.
This is the hour of shadows.

Perhaps in Heraclitus the obscure:

> The one, alone wise, does not and
> does consent to be called by the
> name of Zeus. [9]

Perhaps its expression is to be found in
Father Parmenides. How the Way of Appearance is
related to the Way of Truth is the key for the
understanding his poem. But this catechism
cannot now become a speculative interpretation
of the poem of Parmenides.

Certainly the expression of the unresolved
unity of the Yes-and-No of God in its eternal
submission to the Godhead of God is found in the
eight hypotheses of Plato's Parmenides, properly
understood. The first step towards the proper
understanding of Parmenides is to read it free of
both Neo-Platonic and Hegelian grids by which its
meaning is falsified.

In the very heart of that dark dialogue,
Plato spells out for us the principle of Contradiction:

> ...for the truest assertion of
> the beingness of being and of
> the non-beingness of non-being
> is: when being partakes of the
> beingness of being and not of
> the beingness of non-being --
> that is the fullness of being;
> when non-being does not partake
> of the non-beingness of non-
> being but, rather, of the being-
> ness of non-being -- that is the
> fullness of non-being. [10]

Reasoning which is alive with the Logic of God
follows the principle of Contradiction. The
reasoning which follows from the principle of
non-contradiction (that ghostly derivative at the
heart of Aristotle's Philosophy) is accurate
enough but sickly and pale.

Certainly the expression of the unresolved
unity of the Yes-and-No of God in its eternal
submission to the Godhead of God is found in
Schelling's Ages of the World. Schelling is not
Plato and Plato is not Schelling. Yet they meet
forever in their respective masterpieces.

And yet...

Q16. And yet what?

A16. And yet Dion is assassinated anyway with all
of its cutting sadness and attendant ambiguity.
An attempt to exterminate the Jews remains unap-
preciated with regard to its significance.
Babies are burned. The brightest and most perfect
mirrors are as nothing. The ecstacy of cooperating
most intimately in the revelation of revelation
comes back to haunt and anguish. It would have
been better for man not to have been created at
all says some sacred source.

There is failure built into the very process.

The process is the redemption, as far as is
possible, of the alienated, disintegrated and
externalized character of God. God as eternal
knowledge and truly voluntary does not fail. But
the redemption of God by God with regard to creation remains incomplete if God remains as God. The
disintegration of the alienated nature of God by
which there is creation has the air of finality
about it so long as the godly aspect of God remains
true to itself. In one sense Humpty Dumpty cannot
be put back together again. Divine Plato was, so
to speak, Divine to a fault when he portrayed the
good as a tragic poet (maker). The true theologian
can only agree with Sartre:

> Everything happens as if the
> world, man, and man-in-the-
> world succeeded in realizing
> only a missing God. 11

Q17. Run that by me again, please.

A17. Sartre is not Schelling and Sartre is not
Plato. Nor would the true theologian want to
marry every terminological distinction made by
Sartre. Yet Sartre is the perfect mirror of God
in these words:

> Everything happens as if the
> world, man, and man-in-the-
> world succeeded in realizing
> only a missing God. Everything
> happens therefore as if the
> in-itself and the for-itself
> were presented in a state of
> disintegration in relation to
> an ideal synthesis. Not that
> the integration has ever <u>taken</u>
> <u>place</u> but on the contrary
> precisely because it is always
> indicated and always impossible.
> 12

Q18. Is atheism, then, the only proper expression
of Theology?

A18. In one essential sense, yes. There is no
full revelation of God which does not reveal the
failure of God. Indeed, this tightest and most
grand form of atheism -- Sartre's -- speaks of the
unavoidable failure of what would be -- were it to
occur -- the Divine integration. Even from the
heart of atheism, failed Divinity is still the
appearance of God.

Q19. But is this not worse than no God at all?
A God who intrinsically fails. If failure is the
very standard, who are we -- Sartre's "absurd"
humanism notwithstanding -- to stand up to it?
Along in an absurd meaningless world would seem to
be infinitely preferable to living in a world in

52

which failure is the very standard. Given this
standard of failure, even the pathein-imbued
poet, Baudelaire, seems sophomorically optimistic
in stating:

...all is for the best in the
worst of all possible worlds.[13]

If furthermore, as you have been intimating all
along, our souls are subject to immortality in
a Cosmos in which failure is the very standard,
then despair becomes something like a first
principle for life.

A19. There is still special revelation.

Notes

[6] *Ages of the World*, p. 179.

[7] Cited from *My Sister and I*, allegedly by
Friedrich Nietzsche; allegedly translated by
Oscar Levy; Boar's Head Books, 1951.

[8] *Philebus*; 61.

[9] Heraclitus; fragment #231 as cited in the Kirk
and Raven edition of *The Pre-Socratic Philosophers*.
Variation in translation, my own.

[10] *Parmenides*; from Hypothesis #5.

[11] Sartre. From page 762 of the Barnes translation
of *Being and Nothingness*.

[12] Ibid.

[13] From the end of Charles Baudelaire's *Intimate
Journals*. Translation by Christopher Isherwood.

Introductory Note

to

Chapter Eight

In this essay I confront, directly and
without wincing, the grandest scandal obtaining
in the life of faith. "What is that?", one might
ask. It is this: that Jesus is held hostage by
the Gentile world and that the Jews have not yet
commanded the return of their son who may well be
their unrecognized king.

This chapter is based upon an implied Theology
which I have worked out in the first seven chapters
of Catechism for Theologians. The Theology worked
out there is based upon concepts forged and refined
by the Greek philosopher, Plato, and by the German
philosopher, Schelling. The Theology worked out
in those seven chapters is also compatible with
the God-in-exile motif contained in the various
traditions of Kabbalistic teaching. [14]

I would be surprised if this chapter is found
to be pleasing to Theologians of either Jewish or
Christian persuasion. On the other hand, one does
not write an essay such as this in order to please.
On these matters, one might again cite Elie Wiesel:

> ...Man was created not to know
> happiness but truth. To discover
> it, one must start anew; everything
> must be reviewed. Man, chosen
> by God, must choose Him in turn.
> All ready-made answers, all
> seemingly unalterable certainties

serve only to provide a good
conscience to those who like
to sleep and live peaceably.
To avoid spending a lifetime
tracking down the truth, one
pretends to have found it.
But, so one says in Kotzk,
revelation itself, once it
has become a habit and a
front, becomes suspect.

15

Chapter Eight

SPECIAL REVELATION

Q1. What is special revelation?

A1. It is the free determination of the Godhead
to follow through with all of the consequences
-- bitter or otherwise -- of its gratuitous
victory over other-than-the-free.

The Godhead, even as it is and eternally
becomes and even as it is and becomes eternally
revealed through its relationship with God's
primordial nature, is eternally compromised by
this relationship. It suffers, eternally,
a transformation of what it is -- namely, neither
being nor not being -- by becoming, eternally,
itself. It is other than itself and thus, even
as it reveals itself through its knowledge of
itself, it dies unto itself. Precisely because
it is itself it is no longer what it is.

Accordingly, the only fitting mirror for God
would be a being who pays the unmerited penalty
of death for becoming what it is. It is unmerited
death, more than anything else, by which Adam --
literally in conjunction with Eve -- becomes God-
like and a mirror of and for God. In order for
Adam to become what he is to become -- namely
human, having knowledge of good and evil -- he
must partake of the forbidden fruit. For becoming
what he is to become, Adam pays the unmerited

penalty of death. Nonetheless, the efficient
account of these matters contained in Chapters
Two and Three of Genesis is but the stage setting
for special revelation.

Q2. What is the resolve of God?

A2. The resolve of God is to see the victory of
the Godhead of God through as a victory.

In the redemptive return to the disintegrated
and alienated nature of God, God comes to take a
measure which goes beyond the logic of revelation
brought about by that submission of the primordial
nature of God to the Godhead of God. The logic
of revelation, by itself, only entailed -- only
allowed for -- a partial and necessarily flawed
return to the disintegrated externalization of
God's alienated nature. This extra measure is
compatible with the logic of revelation but is not
required by it. It is freely chosen. God,
special revelation tells us, is not only the truly
voluntary, but also the truly voluntary who also
chooses.

As choice that which is choice in and of God
is other than the truly voluntary even as it is
compatible with the truly voluntary. As choice
this extra measure on the part of God involves
ignorance of outcome. The outcome of God's
coice is not contained in those eternal glimpses
contained in God's knowledge. There is, in
special revelation, risk and no guarantee of
Divine success. On the other hand, it is correct
to say that failure -- with respect to the alienated nature of God -- is the only possible outcome
if this choice is not made.

Q3. If we are now making this distinction between
"choice" in and of God and the "truly voluntary"
of God, ought we not make some preliminary remarks

concerning these and kindred terms?

A3. Yes, keeping in mind that this catechism is
like a circle in as much as, for instance, what
is contained in Chapter Eight informs what is
contained in Chapter One and vice versa.

The whole issue of choice and the voluntary
cries out for a Psychology of behaviour which
would blend the extreme "voluntarism" of a Sartre
with the "knowledge is virtue" doctrine of a
Socrates. Such a blending would fully substanti-
ate common sense notions concerning the voluntary
and the involuntary even though such a blending
would not take its methodological point of depar-
ture from common sense notions of the voluntary
and the involuntary. For these theological
investigations, let the following remarks suffice.

The truly voluntary is desire under conditions
of full knowledge. This is the "normal" posterior
condition of God as has been shown thus far. Thus
God is pure self-determination with respect to
being the eternal end to, of, and for Himself.
In this eternal auto-determination God -- in His
eternal posterior nature -- mimics the utter
indeterminability of the Godhead "prior" to its
victory -- gratuitous in character -- over the
primordial nature of God.

Man approaches the truly voluntary as a limit.
When man acts with full knowledge in every respect
possible, but has ignorance with respect to outcome,
then his action is truly voluntary with respect to
intention, but chosen with respect to outcome.

Choice is desire under conditions of partial
ignorance and partial knowledge. Choice, by
definitionm always involves some degree of
ignorance, at least with respect to outcome,
since outcomes resulting from choice do not occur
without the choice. The "free" process leading
to and including choice is not determined, but it
is motivated.

When the process of choice is motivated by higher and higher levels of knowledge, behaviour approaches the truly voluntary as a limit. The truly voluntary, as such, is both free and voluntary, but does not involve choice.

As behaviour involving some knowledge is motivated more and more by factors other than knowledge, then the behaviour approaches the involuntary as a limit. Choice is the normal condition of man.

The involuntary is that vast complex of action and reaction without the benefit of knowledge. At one extreme it is random chaos. At its other limit it is a complex of end-directed behvaiour, inclusive of passions and desires, which begins to mimic behaviour involving choice. Indeed, man, whose normal behaviour involves choice (i.e., whose normal behavious is performed under conditions of partial ignorance and partial knowledge) biologically arises from the vast network of the involuntary.

Q4. How are these distinctions related to special revelation?

A4. The free is the utterly undetermined and unmotivated Godhead of God prior to its gratuitous victory over the primordial nature of God. The free is compromised and, so to speak, dispersed through this victory. In this sense it is eternally tricked, so to speak, by the primordial nature of God.

The free is present in the eternal posterior character of God as auto-determination which is the truly voluntary in its eternal self-desire. This self-desire is self-knowledge.

The free is present in the human realm involving behaviour under conditions of partial ignorance and partial knowledge.

60

The free -- in its most radically dispersed
form -- is also present in the vast network of
the involuntary. Here the free manifests itself
as that subtle play of mutual determination of
everything by everything. The hierarchical
display of the involuntary -- from randomness
at one extreme to a complex network of end-directed behaviour -- reveals the effect of God's
(presumably) ever-flawed return to His alienated
nature and creation's (presumably) ever-flawed
return to the truly voluntary.

Yet even with this vasr display of revelation,
it is to be kept in mind that the involuntary is
not characterized by knowledge. The bridge
between the involuntary and the truly voluntary
is that realm of action performed under conditions
of partial ignorance and partial knowledge. This
is the human realm of choice.

The truly voluntary is free, auto-determined,
and does not choose. It can choose, but only by
virtue of entering into the realm of ignorance
which, definitionally, at least involves risk with
regard to outcome. If, in point of fact, God does
choose, over and above His voluntary nature, then
God risks His own being as the truly voluntary
since God would then be getting Himself into an
outcome in which the determination does not fully
come from Himself. Therefore, take note of the
following nuance.

God, in His godly nature as truly voluntary,
has no jealousy about Himself and, naturally, so
to speak, freely communicates something of His
own goodness to other than Himself in so far as
that is possible. But God, in His risky choice,
would be a jealous God indeed, very much concerned
with His own vested interest in the outcome of
His choice. Elohim and Yahweh.

Q5. What is the character of God's choice?

A5. As determination for success, the choice is
to risk His eternally revealed nature as knowledge and truly voluntary by doing what is required
to liberate the alienated nature of God back into
the circle of Divine desire without the flaw of
failure. This alienated nature of God, it will be
recalled, already has something of the free --
the Godhead -- in and of it, albeit in radically
compromised form.

There is then, so to speak, a fifth column
already present in the alienated nature of God
capable of responding to any overturn made by God.
God's overture to His alienated nature would not
be sufficient. From the very heart of disintegration a movement back to God would have to be
freely initiated from the side of the alienated
nature of God.

This free response would have to be something
more than that natural erotic response of man
and nature to God's eternal overture as the truly
voluntary. For that circle of desire is necessarily flawed and unsuccessful. The response
would have to be the freely chosen determination
to succeed involving, of course, the risk of total
collapse.

Thus, the re-integration of the alienated
nature of God into the circle of Divine desire
would require a second victory; a second compromise. But this time death must be freely chosen
and not occur as gratuitous compromise. A phrase
for all of this is: the incarnational project in
its two-edged complexity.

Q6. What is incarnation?

A6. It is, in its deepest sense, revelation which
is beyond the eternal logic of revelation and
yet compatible with it. The incarnation of God --
"prior" to special revelation -- eternally occurs
as that disintegrated externalization of the

alienated nature of God. For it is flesh which
is the substantial and symbolic epitome of that
disintegrating externalization.

The chosen incarnation -- which, necessarily,
is posterior to the primeval incarnation -- is the
marriage of God's posterior nature in the most
intimate manner to -- without becoming -- the
disintegrated externalization of God's alienated
nature epitomized by flesh. Thus, from the
perspective of special revelation, there is not
nor can there be an Israel of the spirit which
is not also and simultaneously the Israel of the
flesh.

Q7. Does God become flesh?

A7. Yes and No.

God cannot remain as God and become, freely,
other than God. God in His majestic posterior
nature cannot become flesh without necessarily
losing and destroying that -- God himself -- in
terms of which the success of redemption could
be measured. Redemption would not be worth the
effort if God necessarily destroyed Himself in
the attempt. It is always blasphemous, then, to
maintain that God has become flesh. The test of
true revelation is whether or not it implies --
or states -- this blasphemy.

However, God could remain as God if the flesh
-- calling upon the free (compromised) Godhead
held hostage, so to speak, by and in the alienated
nature of God -- were to choose to become God.
Indeed, re-integration must fail and be eternally
flawed unless the free overture from the side of
God is met with an actively free initiative from
the side of creation.

How to elicit this free response on the part
of the flesh? God, in and through the incarnational project, would have to position Himself,

so to speak. He would have to set the stage for
a grand drama, played out be the representatives
of the flesh over their entire history, by which
the flesh freely chooses to re-integrate itself
without flaw into the circle of Divine desire.

Q8. Please outline in sketch form the complexity
of this two-edged incarnational project. Then
I might ask you to clarify some of the details.

A8. First and foremost is the Covenant of God
with the Jews.

The Covenant with the Jews is that the Jews,
as a people and according to the rites of the
flesh, be the vehicle of and for God's special
revelation. The Jews, in a sense, are the embo-
diement of God. To aid in and for the successful
outcome of redemption history, information and
guiding revelation, in the form of Torah, was
given to this people through several avenues.
Torah was to be continually tested and refined as
the project of revelation unfolded itself.

The chosen-ness of this people with regard to
the incarnational project -- not fully revealed
in advance since it would have to be freely
chosen -- set up within this people a tension
with regard to its fulfillment. The chosen-ness
of this people with regard to the incarnational
project would at some time require that some one
Jew -- since choice is quintessentially individual
on the part of the one who chooses -- would have
to choose, freely, to become God. For being God
-- given the character of God -- can only occur
through a free act. The anxiety of this choice
would be almost unendurable since the choice,
once made, would be unique and could not be
undone.

This man would have to bring further understanding to his people about their incarnational
mission and self-understanding. He would bring

this understanding both through his teachings
and through his life, suffering and death. Both
is symbol and in substance he would have to freely
undergo the extreme of unmerited disintegration
for the sake of ultimate re-integration.

With the choice of "Yahweh saves" ("Yahweh
delivers") the Covenant reaches a critical stage.
God chooses the Jews through Abraham and Moses.
The Jews choose God through the free election of
Jesus.

The disintegration of Jesus is complete.
Beyond the misunderstandings, the whipping, the
nailing; beyond the rendering of the flesh;
beyond all of that there is psychological disintegration. There is the moment of despair.
Drawing on the experience of his own people, Jesus
cites Scripture and cries out -- to himself in a
sense -- "My God, my God, why have you abandoned
me?" 16

There has been much misunderstanding about
this person. Much of the misunderstanding about
this person was ensconced in the set of sacred
writings by which the reports on the life, ministry,
passion and death of Jesus are passed on to the
generations.

The greatest misunderstanding about this man
comes forth as the foolish notion that with this
man redemption history no longer has an essential
connection with the Jews. Quite to the contrary,
God's covenant with the Jews is sealed in forever
with this Jew's choice to be God. Thus, there
is no redemption which does not occur through the
agency of the Jewish people.

Q9. What is Torah?

A9. Torah is multi-faceted.

It is the story of exile and the return from

65

exile. As such it is a hint and a revelation concerning the very structure of God.

From beginning to end Torah is the invitation to excercise freedom. It is the invitation to become what one is to become even if the price is most dear. Yet, simultaneously, Torah is that invitation to engage in the risk of freedom in such a manner that one increases rather than diminishes the probability of success in the outcome. This is why Torah is called Law.

Freedom without Law squanders itself in a useless passion. Still, the Law dimension of Torah is for the sake of freedom. Freedom is not for the sake of the Law dimension of Torah. The Jew, Jesus, was perfectly attuned to thie tension (freedom-Law-freedom) which is Torah. He teaches this tension to his people.

Torah is best exemplified in the story of Exodus.

How, through the jealousy of his brothers in Judaism, Joseph was exiled, in bondage, into the land of Egypt.

How Joesph, surprisingly enough, came to prosper in the land of Egypt.

How, amazingly soon afterwards, necessity forced the father and brothers of Joseph out of their homeland and into the land of Egypt.

How, over time, the descendants of Joseph and his brothers became degraded slaves in the land of Egypt.

How the free response of one man to a special overture on the part of God was the catalyst by which liberation was finally achieved.

How the people, freely, did and did not accept the leadership of Moses.

How there was a great time-lag -- and much
testing -- between the free decision of Moses and
the final deliverance to the Homeland.

How, even after the journey was completed,
entrance to the Homeland was not achieved without
struggle.

How Moses suffered although he was the catalyst
for liberation.

How God freely invites and how man must --
with great risk to all that he holds dear --
freely respond.

It is the story of God's relationship to His
people.

The grand Exodus, however, is still to be
played out.

Jesus is Joseph and Moses at once, in approx-
imate reverse order. With Joseph there is exile.
With Moses there is anguished choice, leading to
liberation and return.

With Jesus there is the anguished choice
followed by his exile (through Paul) into the
lands of the Gentiles. The Jews follow Jesus
into exile soon after with the destruction of the
Temple. Jesus is, surprisingly enough, well
received in the lands of the Gentiles. Over time,
the people of God come to be degraded and perse-
cuted in the lands of the Gentiles. The return
of the Jews to Israel now brings with it -- in
symbol and in substance -- the conditions under
which the Jews, freely, do or do not endorse, for
all eternity, the choice made in their name of the
Son of Man to become God.

The choice has been made by Jesus. Now, as
we approach the fullness of time, will the chosen
people respond and freely endorse this choice,
thereby bringing the incarnational project full
circle? The choice of Jesus is, in effect, the

choice of the Godhead held hostage in the alienated nature of God. But God's Covenant is with
the Jews as a people and it is only through the
Jews as a people that the circle of the incarnational project can be completed.

All non-Jews are but spectators -- some of
whom (especially those Christians who believe
that slavation is an accomplished fact) being
unknowing spectators -- in the grand drama of
decision being played out by the Jews for all of
mankind -- and for all Nature as well. To
interfere in this decision in such a manner to
impede the freeness of this decision would be
foolish and self-destructive. But we can urge
and cheer them on.

Q10. What about the New Testament?

A10. It is not Torah. Indeed, in order for the
Jews to freely accept and endorse the choice of
Jesus, it is essential that this choice not be
revealed through Torah. The invitation to exer-
cise freedom which is Torah requires that the Jews,
at some poinr, take the risk of going out into
ignorance. In the realm of special revelation,
to go out into ignorance is to go outside of Torah.

No, the New Testament is not Torah at all.
It is at its best a concatenation of misunderstandings. At its worst it is a concatentation of
hatred, prejudice, resentiment and self-pity
dressed up as the Gospel of love. It is, however,
sacred and the vehicle by which -- even in the
heart of misunderstanding -- the choice of Jesus
is conveyed over the ages. The exile of Jesus
into the lands of the Gentiles brings with it holy
writings which misrepresent the person and mission
of Jesus even as those writings convey, despite
themselves, what they positively reveal about
Jesus.

With St. Paul, the essential step of exile
is taken which takes Jesus out of his homeland
and away from his people.

With the fourth Gospel the extreme of exile
is accomplished in two ways.

In the first place, in this Gospel, Jesus
is thematically contrasted with "the Jews" even
though -- unbeknownst to the author(s) of the
fourth Gospel -- the choice of Jesus can be
successful in its outcome if and only if the
choice is ratified, freely, by the Jews.

In the second place, in this Gospel, the choice
of Jesus to become God is blasphemously misconstrued into the choice of God to become man. The
very mission of Jesus is exiled from its proper
understanding.

Yet this exile of Jesus into the lands of the
Gentiles (largely accomplished by the New Testament writings) is itself part of the backdrop by
which the choice of Jesus can be understood over
the fullness of time. In a kind of perverted way,
these writings, alone, do transmit, despite themselves, the choice of Jesus. This is the anguished
choice by which the Son of Man -- who is no more
or less the Son of God than you or I -- became
God. If you stand outside of the Covenant, the
meaning of this choice necessarily remains hidden.
Even from within the Covenant, the meaning of this
choice remains hidden thus far.

Q11. What about the judgement of the Sanhedrin?

A11. If a man claims that God has become man, he
blasphemes. For God is other than man. God cannot
become man and remain as God. The incarnation is
badly misconstrued if it is understood in this
fashion. The teaching of the incarnation in this
fashion is blasphemous and the judgement of the
Sanhedrin is sustained.

The Divine incarnational project can success-
fully complete itself only if, under the right
conditions -- (viz., from within the Covenant) --
man freely chooses to be and become God. Then and
only then can God remain as God and the alienated
nature of God be returned -- without flaw -- into
the circle of Divine desire.

Choice is by its nature individual. Thus the
choice involved in this case is the anguished
choice of one man for all. Such a decision -- if
it is not the decision of a psychopath -- can only
emerge from a deep understanding of God's Covenant
with the Jews. Such a choice is the response of
a Jew for the Jews. No one alive during the time
of Jesus could have been expected to have understood the direction from which Jesus was coming in
his intimations, before the Sanhedrin, about his
authority and Divinity. Indeed, it seems that only
the anguished thinking about the Covenant occas-
ioned by the Holocaust could bring this dimension
of Jesus to light. Daughters of Jerusalem, weep
for yourselves and your children. To be among
the chosen people is an honor and a burden.

The writers of the New Testament -- in the
variety of ways by which they misconstrued the
centrality of Jesus -- no more understood Jesus
than did the Sanhedrin as it found Jesus guilty
of blasphemy. Further, the Theology commensurate
with the mistaken portrayal of Jesus in the New
Testament, ironically enough, leads further away
from an understanding of Jesus.

In contrast, the judgement of blasphemy made
by the Sanhedrin does, by a curious route, lead
-- if one meditates sufficiently long on the
evidence -- to an unraveling of the freely chosen
drama consciously played out by Jesus during his
week in Jerusalem. Jesus -- if you read what the
four Gospels reveal about that week in Jerusalem
despite the intent of their authors -- did nothing
less than orchestrate his own dramatic death. In
particular, the manner of his own self-defense
before the Sanhedrin forced the hand of the priests

and elders. In doing all of this Jesus is not at all a psychopath. Rather, he is playing out and sealing in his momentous choice. The king must die.

If God becomes man, then the very conditions for success in God's incarnational project are destroyed in a blasphemous act of needless self-destruction perpetrated by God himself. But if a man chose to respond freely to that unique invitation by God to become God, then is set in motion the train of events which would enable the successful return of the alienated nature of God back, without flaw, into the circle of Divine desire.

Q12. Can the Covenant of God with the Jews be broken?

A12. If and when the Jews disappear as a people, then not only will the Covenant be broken, but the Divine risk for redemption and victory will have been lost. And the strength of that Covenant has been seriously tested in our own century.

There is reason for hope. The Jews have re-established themselves in the land of Israel. The time of victory may be at hand, for it is unlikely that the Jews can disappear as a people except by virtue of the destruction of mankind itself. Such mass destruction is presumably the start of the final re-integration -- if it is to occur at all -- since Adam must die as mankind as well as die as each individual. Of course if the final destruction is to be the beginning of re-integration, then the Jews must accept and ratify the Messiah.

Q13. Who is the Messiah?

A13. Jesus of Nazareth who seals in forever the incarnational project of God through the Jews. For Jews to accept Jesus as the Messiah is any-

71

thing but for Jews to be converted to any variety of Christianity. For Jews to accept Jesus as the Messiah is for the Jews -- each individually and in that fashion collectively as well -- to make a final assessment of themselves as a people. They will discover to the full measure their Divine nature.

The Messianic expectation is historical.

The history of this expectation first creates that tension which culminates in the choice of Jesus -- from within the Covenant -- to become God. The exile of Jesus into the Gentile world sets the conditions under which the incarnational project can be brought to completing. The rescue of God, as Jesus, from exile on this level ignites the process by which God, finally, rescues His own alienated nature from exile.

Accordingly, the Messianic expectation on the part of the Jews after the time of Jesus is a kind of unconscious expression of their internal anxiety concerning that return from exile which will usher in the cosmic return from exile of God's alienated nature back, without flaw, into the circle of Divine desire. Jesus, so to speak, must be rescued from his exile in the lands of the Gentiles and returned to his home within the Covenant for all of this to take place.

Christians, therefore, if they are faithful to Jesus, can be followers of Jesus only by literally becoming Jewish. Since God's covenant with the Jews is one according to the, flesh, the hope and plan of Christians who see the light is to be born of a Jewish mother in some future incarnation of their souls.

Q14. Then special revelation is, at bottom, the Jewish people themselves?

A14. Yes. Its success as revelation basically

requires two conditions. In the first place, the
continuation of the Jewish people, as a people,
until the end of mankind's history. In the second
place, the full acceptance of the Jewish people,
by the Jewish people, of their nature and function.
This acceptance entails the acceptance of Jesus as
the Messiah and, through their acceptance of Jesus,
their acceptance of themselves -- in the non-blas-
phemous manner outlines in this Chapter -- as the
incarnated presence of God in redemptive history.
This acceptance would be the catalyst for the
re-integration of the alienated nature of God,
back into,without flaw, the circle of Divine desire.

Thus special revelation -- which aims only at
final success -- need not be appreciated by anyone,
least of all by anyone not in the Jewish Covenant.
It need only succeed. It remains compatible with
general revelation. From all directions everything
shouts out, silently: let God become what He is:
Victory.

Q15. What, with slightly more precision, does the
re-integration of the alienated nature of God
back into the flawless circle of Divine desire
entail?

A15. Approximately this.

In the logic of general revelation the non-
jealous communication of God's goodness over to
His alienated nature brings with it the demiurgic
generation of individual souls largely divine in
their make-up. However, even as the alienated
nature of God responds to the overture of God,
the whirlpool of disintegration as it externalizes
brings about a kind of cosmic spiral drag the logic
of which is maximal and finalized externalization.
Souls can and do get caught in this spiral drag.
The outcome of total and final externalization
would seal in forever the failure of God.

However, it is theoretically possible that

73

the concentration of the Divine in souls could reverse the direction of the spiral drag if they were to position themselves, so to speak, to benefit directly from the overtures of God. This drama of positioning has been going on for a long time by the way in which souls take on human form according to God's Covenant with the flesh.

If the positioning is successful, then the stage is (will have been) set for a Divine connection powerful enough to shake the heavens and reverse the direction of the spiral drag. At the upper end of that spiral would then be the community of souls brought in directly to the circle of Divine desire.

Q16. If the time of victory is possibly at hand, then are we in the last days?

A16. As with fig trees, so too with the signs of the times.

There is the in-gathering of the Jews back to Israel in our time. This is an event which would have been thought absolutely impossible a half-century ago except for some dreamers.

Similarly, a kind of in-gathering of souls back to Mother Earth is occurring with an exponential suddenness. It is not unlike the coming together of family on the last holiday before some family member dies. It is time for the whole family to die? Are we in-gathered for our own nostalgic good-bye? Also, it is possible that all souls must be present in the flesh at the end of time.

Momentous events quite possibly happen in two-thousand year cycles. Saturn and Jupiter -- the "wanderers" symbolic of changing kingship -- were uniquely aligned the year in which Jesus was born. Now, interestingly enough, Pluto -- the "wanderer" symbolic of the dead -- comes closer

74

for a short visit of about twenty years before it
resumes its role as outermost "wanderer".

America and Russia emerge as the Gog and
Magog of Godlessness capable of precipitating
the destruction of mankind.

Then there is the sign and warning given
through the anguish of the Holocaust. Writers
who have lived through the Holocaust hint that
there was something irreversible which occurred
through those darkest years.

Also, the appearance of false Messiahs.

On the other hand, there are no signs whatsoever that mainstream Judaism is about to accept
Jesus as the Messiah. On the other hand again,
there is no guarantee that God's risky choice for
redemption through the agency of the Jewish people
is to be successful. The end could come without
the completion of the circle -- through the Jews
-- of God's redemptive incarnational project.

In any case, there is always reason to doubt
that one is in the eschatological age. The near-
ness of the end has always emerged as a theme in
human history and so far it has not come to pass.
In difficult times those who are cowardly and
lacking is perseverance have usually become
enamoured at the thought of living in the time of
the eschaton.

The true deduction to be made from the signs
of the times is the following. Whether or not
these are the last days, we must live our lives
in accordance with the exigencies of general
revelation and the exigencies of special revelation in their mutual support of each other.
No more; no less.

Notes

[14] For the way in which these theological investigations are grounded in Plato and Schelling, one would have to consult the first seven chapters of this work. The writer of this essay has but a popular and indirect knowledge of Kabbalistic teaching based on the relevant writings of Elie Wiesel and Gershom Scholem.

[15] Cited from *Souls on Fire* by Elie Wiesel; Randon House, New York, 1972; p. 241.

[16] Cited from Chapter 27 of *St. Matthew's Gospel*.